Feeling everything

Jemma McConville-Roe

BookLeaf Publishing

Presentation by *BookLeaf Publishing*

Web: www.bookleafpub.com

E-mail: info@bookleafpub.com

ISBN: 9789357444514

First edition 2023

To George, Rio and Martha

I did a thing!

and to Mama - I miss you

Always x

PREFACE

I started writing poetry after realising reading poetry was what I always turned to when I needed an escape from the chatter of my particularly noisy and sometimes quite mean internal monologue.

I often find committing to sitting quietly and reading a book overwhelming, you can always see exactly how far you still have to go. You can however always find a poem to read that is as short or long as you need, and each one is it's own individual little adventure for your head and heart.

I have always been an emotional person, and I haven't always known how to manage that in a way that wasn't all or nothing. As a bit of an emotional yo yo I could always find so much joy, awe, wonder in being human, but inevitably always close by was sadness, loss and sorrow - and it would overpower me.

I wrote these poems at a time when I was starting on journey of learning balance. They represent my growth in being able to appreciate all the things I have and how I have started to use my emotional responses as tools for my growth. I have always felt it is important to share the parts of you that you are typically taught to hide.

I hope it encourages you to hide a little less.

An Introduction

About me… (where should I start?)
5ft 5, weight unknown
Big heart
Own body fearer (now a thing much less feared)
Kind
Kind of funny
Kind of silly
Kind of weird
Positively always half a glass full
…or empty
…or kicked over and scrambling for a tea towel
to mop up the mess
Oversharer (my super power!!)
Overthinker (my kryptonite)
Feminist, fighter, woman gone wild
Resilient, strong (read: stubborn as a child)
Like a joyous sonata played allegra, in the key
of G major,
but with the odd accidental B minor,
A strong piano tune
A racing violin
But with a bit of quirky primary school recorder
lesson thrown in for good measure.
Not much of a hugger, but empathetic to a fault.
Honest

P

O

E

T

In the Wardrobe

I'm never going to wear you,
even though you've been in there a while.

Even though you are cosy, I'm never going to
wear you,
But I'll think often about how you wrapped
small bones, pale skin,
...always cold, always in layers.

I'm never going to wear you, even though
you smell only of the wardrobe now.
Not bright Sunflowers, or dark heavy Obsession
...that kitchen.

It's not even that you are not my colour,
I'm usually strewn in pops of purple, pink,
yellow, green -
I could wrap myself in beige, it's not that,
...I'm just never going to wear you.

It's not even because seeing you scared me,
Or that when you came home you made me cry,
Or that I have no exact specific memory of you,
to remind me.

I’m just …never going to wear you,
even though you are hanging there, waiting to warm someone,
because that's what jumpers do.

I’ll never wear you, Mum’s jumper.

I’m just going to hang you up in the wardrobe,
And get warmth from knowing you are there.

How I feel things ... part one

Gosh I get so angry sometimes

It starts in my stomach, slowly
crawling
upwards, rising
in temperature
Until it hits my heart and fervidly runs through
every vein,
every capillary,
like scalding running water
filling a bath right to the brim

And then starts the drip,
drip, drip,
drip
before it all cascades out,
in a flood of words, gestures and red hot tears.
And I stand there lucent,
wondering what to do next.

They start teaching you young....

School Dress Code

Girls
Shirt buttons must be done up
Trousers must be smart, and fitted, but not form fitting
Socks must cover ankles
Shirt sleeves must meet your wrist
PE T-shirt sleeves must be at least 3 fingers wide, there can be no shoulder on show.
Tie must be worn
Shirts must be the correct thickness, there must be absolutely no visibility of your bra.
No jewellery
Hair must be clean, well groomed and no odd hair colours permitted.
No shorts more than 0.5cms above the knee, there will be measuring
No skirts above the knee
No skirts
Clothing must in no way call attention to the natural shape of your growing body
Please remember you will be looked at at all times

Please remember you are a distraction
Please internalise the early trauma of this scrutiny
Please remember you are no more than a body
Tests on this subject matter will continue for the rest of your life

Boys
Tie must be worn

Why do I write?

I write because I have quite nice handwriting,
and then I type it up because everything is
modern these days.
And I feel a bit sad that nobody gets to see my
handwriting,
but that is just the way of the world now.
And it's a shame, because I spent a lot of time
on that handwriting,
when I was younger, every school report was,
"she is excellent at the topic but she really needs
to work on that handwriting".
So I worked on it
and now hardly anyone that isn't me, gets to see
it.

Because I am emotional
and when it comes out of my mouth in words, it
dunt sound so good…
Yet on paper the same words can sound really
beautiful.
So I write because emotion is beautiful, and
human and special,
and I want to share that with people,
I want them to say "hey that was pretty special
and I felt that way once".

And then they will hopefully think for a bit and
they'll realise "wow I'm special too",
and maybe they will spread the word, emotion is
beautiful, and human, and special,
and one day I will read about it in someone
else's poem and I'll bathe in the serendipity.

Because sometimes I need a break from my
brain.
My never ending internal monologue.
Do this, do that, you did this, you did that,
that was very silly, now feel a certain way about
it.
It's very bossy, I need to give it something else
to do.
So I write it out,
I put it down on paper,
Shhhhhhhh....
Silence
And then later on I look back and I think "wow,
that really was very silly."
Very Silly of me to listen to such nonsense from
my brain,
and I smile and I feel my growth.

I write because I actually feel like I am good at it
But I want to get better.
I often stress that getting better means simply
getting wordier.

Writing all in similes and metaphors,
descriptively describing everything beautifully.
And then people will read it and they are like
"wow",
"wasn't that just full of imagery… I think I get
it".
And it can ultimately mean to them whatever
they need it to.
But I also write because I am honest,
Well emotion is truly honest isn't it?
And honest words don't really need making
pretty
So maybe I can just write that other way
sometimes.

I write because someone like you will read it,
and I am very glad that you have.
It has made my heart very happy.
I wish I had written for you sooner.

My Ritual

I relish the early morning
Every one changes slightly with the seasons
The rising or not yet so risen sun
The birds chorus
Dew through to frost
That secret time between just me and what is to
come.
There's something special about knowing that
you are one of the first.

So I'll savour my tea
The steam waking up my sleepy face.
Light a few candles
Write a few words
Whisper to the universe, this is going to be a
good day, this is going to be a really good day
And hope that it reciprocates the message.

I'd take a thousand of those mornings over a
grand adventure

How i feel things ... part two

An often conversation with my brain.

“What emotions do we have today?”
“Many, an almost never ending list in fact, and you can have them all”
“In tandem?”
“Simultaneously”

My body sighs and steels itself again.

Marriage

You're such a weirdo.
You really are strange
and the way you behave is well … odd
And oddly I often wonder
what is going through your head.

And I roll my eyes, and I say
jeez you are strange
And I carry on with what I was trying to do and
so do you.

You can be very annoying.
You don't listen when I say,
stop that.
Probably because I am suppressing a laugh,
and you like to make me laugh
….and I like that too

Then I'll have things to do,
and so do you really,
so it'll be "Until next time!"
and the next time won't be far away.

You’re kind of kooky.
You mess around alot.
and you say things and they make no sense.
And I smile and say something like “We could never go on Gogglebox”

But I think if other people heard them,
they wouldn’t understand.
They’d look all confused and they’d say
“What?”
because you are such a weirdo.
But I am too.
So that worked out.

Haiku

Grief like deep winter
or the searing of summer
spring never quite arrives...

How I feel things ... part three

Sometimes I experience such intense feelings of joy
They rush in like a tornado
Vertical tunnels rapidly spinning their way through the storm in my body
Lifting my heart high above the clouds.

In the peace that comes after I idly reflect on what I did to deserve such a marvel
And the answer is simply that I exist.

My Voice

The colour of yellow like the warmth of the sun,
growing in strength as the day goes on.
The sun on an early spring day, sometimes it
feels cooler,
sometimes it's bright
Sometimes things will come along and hide it ,
a cloud,
some rain,
A long and stormy night,
it takes that moment to hide, to question, before
appearing again.
Always returning.

Like a small bird or maybe a bird that's been
injured,
stepping out.
Tentative, hoping to once again take flight.
And then it does,
it's soaring in the thermals
riding the highs and lows
instinctively.
And the sun bursts through the clouds,
and its wings reveal astonishing colours

It’s slow and soft with undertones of child,
excitement.
Like that child who quite accidentally,
realised they could do something for the first
time.
A child that is learning to walk,
leaning into those steps, learning their feeling,
learning their balance,
bold, daring, with great aplomb.

And it is running, head first, ready to greet what
is waiting for it.

Topography

I
really love
Mountains
They fill me with absolute awe.
Mother Nature's intoxicating giants.
Their scale is often completely unfathomable.
I know I am not alone in this feeling, maybe it's
an evolutionary quirk.
Or maybe it is that you are the centre of your
own universe, the biggest thing in your world
But next to a mountain you can finally take a
breath and realise that you really are quite small.
Or is it that they are really just imperfections (in
the earth's crust) that have found a way to
remain beautiful,
and that somehow, that resonates inside you too.
Even if it doesn't, I hope it's a simile that makes
you smile.

As I watch her I think...

Dance like nobody's watching my beautiful child, every day, as you grow, anywhere you can.

Because even if they are it is with envy in their eyes and a raging emerald green jealousy in their hearts.
Overwhelmed, overworked and consumed by carrying the weight of other people's expectations.
Their muscles screaming from constantly suppressing that instinctive urge to just seek joy.
They can never be dancers.

Dancers are wild souls,
Spirited, effervescent, full of starlight,
They are light and nimble, yet they manage to move mountains effortlessly.
They are driven by authenticity, defiant against conformity

I am so proud I raised a dancer

The Other

Aren't we all the same?
All flesh and bone
All breath and beat

Don't we all come home
After a long day, just wanting to rest
Cradle our child in close to our breast

Eat a nice meal
Kiss husband, wife, partner, mother, father

Don't we all crave warmth?

Even though we weren't born in the same land
Even though some lives aren't as grand
Aren't we all the same?
All flesh and bone
All breath and beat

Don't tell me you wouldn't put your child in a
boat, and pray
to somebody, it's going to float
Wouldn't we all want to be safe - to be afforded
some peace in a quieter place

Eat a nice meal
Kiss husband, wife, partner, mother, father

Wouldn't we all walk those thousand of miles
in genuine need
To only be turned away
To many to feed
What are your reasons?
Don't we all crave warmth
After a long day day, just wanting to rest
And cradle our child in close to our breast

Aren't we all the same?
We'd do all that we could
Struggle through the fear and the pain and the mud
Hiding the blood
Ears ringing - a city of bombs
to be afforded some safe in a quieter place
Cradle our child in close to our breast
Wanting to rest
Our flesh, Our bones,
Our breath, Our beat.

Presence

A life blurred,
perfectionism its curse,
bound to finding the tiniest of faults,
oblivious to any of its power,
joy entirely thieved by comparison

A life taken back,
by the simple recognition,
that power can be found simply in being,
not perfect,
just present.

Irreplaceable

Small hands grasping at me,
Never getting a hot cup of tea
The brush of a curl
The stroke of a head
The weight of a body carried to bed
Making them laugh the sweetest little giggle
A million new nicknames, my button, my pickle

The way that their big eyes lovingly stare,
Snuggles with blankets on the sofa or a chair
The very first time they pair paper and paint
That look of not me! I couldn't! I'm a saint!
Seeing them learning
Both fast and slow
Watching a personality blossom and grow.

Twenty minutes of cleaning, for a five minute meal,
Endless time trying to guess what they feel,
Tearing your hair out by the end of the day,
Watching them sleep, it all goes away,
Unconditional love, unwavering trust
Your heart feels like it may just want to combust

Never getting a solo trip to the loo
Or the kitchen, or to bed or the bath too
Knowing you never knew tired until now.
That you're keeping them alive but you’re not quite sure how.
It’s the hardest of times,
But unmatched in every way
Irreplaceable
Cherish every day

Enough

Exactly how much time I wasted trying to change myself, I have no idea

Never for one second beleiveing I had anything of worth.

Oscillating wildly through self hate, self criticism , self improvement

Until finally one day

Gathering all my strength, I gave voice to the idea that maybe the only self I needed was myself.

Happiness arrived when I realised. I am…..

Sorrow

I often think of sorrow like water
They are similar in many ways
Both can start to make their presence known
with a slow…
Drip,drip, drip
Penetrating any crevice,
Even the tiniest pinhole,
Taking any path that will assist its downward
flow,
As consistent as gravity,
Finding the lowest level with remarkable
efficiency,
Then slowly filling the space it has found to
settle in.
It's soft stream sounds comforting at first,
And it's weight feels sustainable,
Until, like a jug filled just one drop too far,
It begins to trickle,
Before cascading vociferously over the edge,
Running like a river,
Winding it's way over the terrain,
Creating new boundaries,
Forcing new paths
Mercurial in it's temperament

Washing away anything that stands irresolutely in its path.
And it feeds,
Joined by tributaries from places long forgotten
Swelling, not only in size, but velocity and turbulence,
Only quelled once it reaches the sea.
Where there is an opportunity for lifeboats,
To take those ensnarled, back to the safety of the shore.

Luck

I sit there across from you, warm cup of tea
clasped between my hands.
The slanting sunlight creeping between us, turns
your drink's steam into a fountain of gold glitter,
before draping off the table,
and you are telling me stories.
Your words buzz around my ears, and I am
watching you intently
but none of their meaning is really registering,
it's just a soft babble in the welcome tone of
your voice.
I am distracted, but not for once by anything
disquieting,
I have just been struck by a feeling.
That gosh I am so lucky.
Lucky that my soul got to walk the earth at the
same time as yours.

Life

As the saying goes - the sun will always rise.
ever dependable, starting each day with it's slow
crawl,
upwards, reaching out it's rays
an announcement of life continuing.

And as its light shines down on the world
a wonderful harmony begins,
where every branch, flower, insect, animal,
person
begins to cast their shadow,
A beautiful kaleidoscope of patterns, never two
the same
An announcement of their lives also.

www.ingramcontent.com/pod-product-compliance
Lightning Source LLC
Chambersburg PA
CBHW051750130826
49812CB00033B/1082
* 9 7 8 9 3 5 7 4 4 4 5 1 4 *